DA VINCI
THE PAINTER WHO SPOKE WITH BIRDS

CONTENTS

The Painter Who Spoke with Birds   6

Chronology   60

Photographic Credits   61

Glossary   62

Cover: *The Virgin and Child with Saint Anne,*
Louvre Museum, Paris. Photo: Scala

Graphic design: Sandra Brys (Zig-Zag)

First published in the United States in 1994 by
Chelsea House Publishers.

© 1993 by Casterman, Tournai

First Printing

1 3 5 7 9 8 6 4 2

ISBN 0-7910-2808-9

ART FOR CHILDREN

DA VINCI

THE PAINTER WHO SPOKE WITH BIRDS

By Yves Pinguilly

Translated by John Goodman

CHELSEA HOUSE PUBLISHERS

NEW YORK • PHILADELPHIA

To: Mr. Léopold Telliére
19 Dinterville Street
Paris, France

Dear Uncle,

*T*he weather is beautiful. I'm in the garden. The sky is blue. The sun is right in the middle of the sky, and it looks like a fried egg. You'll never guess what's happened to me! Now you'll have another reason to say I'm as crazy as they come. Here goes: I went with my class to Chanteloup-des-Neiges for two weeks. I suppose you might say I was in snow class. I skied up a storm there. Anyone will vouch for me. For hours at a time I was Queen of the Snow. That's really what I felt like. But one morning there was a thin layer of ice over the course, and I went flying. The terrible thing about flying off like that is you have to come back down! Well, the long and the short of it is, I broke both my legs. It's pretty rare for one person to have two broken legs. I'll just have to be patient until late spring, when I should be able to walk as well as before. I'm all plastered up, but I'm not writing to tell you the story of my life. I'm writing because you're a poet who knows everything, and I'm launching an investigation.

I've decided to make you my sole, my principal, my unique witness in this investigation. It concerns a painter: LEONARDO DA VINCI.

I'm investigating him because of his painting of *Mona Lisa*. In my room at the hospital the *Mona Lisa* was hanging on the wall. I went to sleep and woke up with her for two days and nights. I even recited a poem to her that you wrote for me when I was little, the one that begins:

Crazy Rose
Rosa ring
Ring around the rosy
Funny hat
What a cat
Gotcha in the whatsy

She smiled when I talked to her. I want to know more about this lady who kept me company and who has become my friend.

I also want to know more about the painter, this Leonardo da Vinci. Do people call him Leo, like you? When did he live?

If you don't help me out with some answers, then when I'm all well I'll come to see you and be as mean as possible. Answer my queries, you who know everything. I've promised everyone to learn a thousand things in my spring garden. For several weeks, it's the garden that will be my school.

Best wishes.
Rosa

To: Miss Rosa Telliére
Villa on the Point
Val-Lilas, France

Rosa my Rose,

What luck! You have two broken legs, so you don't ask me to dance but write to me instead. What luck, you've chosen to investigate one of the greatest of all human geniuses, Leonardo da Vinci. As far as I know no one called him Leo. But some called him "master." I'll be glad to tell you about Leonardo, a painter who was much more than a painter. While you're quietly waiting in your garden for your legs to heal, open your eyes—the windows of your soul—and look around you. Look carefully, and you'll see that the harmony of nature is meaningful. This innocent harmony was always Leonardo's companion and model. As a painter, he wanted to bring men and forms into the world. Through his art, he revealed to men and women their reason, their hearts, and the manifold beauty within the world's encompassing unity. He tried to expose the presence of this beauty deep within every one of us by painting faces caressed by soft light.

I will do my best to answer your questions.

The limits of our lives are set by a horizon. This horizon is a boundary that can be pushed back by love and art. When you think you've grown up, love will come along and deepen your experience. You'll see. But at this point, art can already enlighten you and chase away some of your fears. Leonardo's painting in particular depicts men and women who are "reborn" in the world. If examined closely, it can help you to get your bearings. It's like a mirror bringing you into the world. Allow yourself to be born and reborn. Believe me, both love and art exist to increase the maturity of human beings. Use your eyes well. Careful examination of a painting by Leonardo of Florence can deepen self-understanding, making it stronger and more far-reaching.

Yes, I'm going to answer your first question. The painter of the *Mona Lisa* lived during the Renaissance. Tomorrow I'll write you about what that means.

Best wishes to my malicious niece and her two broken legs.

Your uncle Leo

P.S. (All real letters must have a postscript.) Here is a closing gift in the form of a saying by Master Leonardo. It seems relevant to your present circumstances: "Iron rusts when it's not used; stagnant water loses its purity and freezes in the cold. Similarly, lack of activity saps the mind's vigor."

Rosa my Rose of the Winds,

Today I call you my Rose of the Winds because the wind blowing constantly from north to south and east to west is much luckier than you, stuck as you are in one place with your casts. You can't move very far, but you can dream. And I'm not so sure the wind can do that.

My Rose of the Winds, if you were indeed the wind you could go to Brittany and see the thick-walled chateau of Duchess Anne. You could fly to Angers and see the chateau of the good king Rene with its battlements. These fortified buildings are medieval structures.

And you could also see the Chateau of Blois further upstream on the banks of the Loire River, with its beautiful Renaissance staircase devised by a fantastic architectural imagination; and since fluttering about is very like dancing, you'd have to go to Fontainebleau to see the ballroom there. These beautiful 16th-century structures would make you want to see more, and then you'd blow yourself to Flanders, where Bruges awaits you, and then to Italy and the city of Urbino, and on to Florence.

Florence!

The Renaissance began in the West around the year 1400, when virtually all of the people living in this part of the world were Christian. The Renaissance drew to a close—after 1,000 discoveries, inventions, and dreams—some 200 years later.

The Renaissance swept away the Middle Ages. Suddenly, men realized they could understand the world and judge it as well. They wanted to seize for themselves some of the power attributed to God. They wanted to place themselves at the center of the universe. In fact, you might say that the men of this era invented reason even though they kept their faith. Standing up to the gods who had previously reigned unchallenged, they became more audacious and less faithful, less deferential. These were new men, free of long-standing prejudices. In this period, nature was the primary source of knowledge. Artists, engineers, and peasants alike observed it carefully.

A residence
in Bruges built
during the Renaissance.

The Chateau of
Azay-le-Rideau, erected
at the beginning of
the 16th century, is one
of the most beautiful
chateaux of the French
Renaissance.

This was the beginning of modern science. Research was undertaken and experiments were carried out. Things that could be confirmed by the senses were held in high esteem. If men developed new ideas, this was not by chance; it wasn't magic. You should know, my Rose of the Winds, that more and more of the earth's surface was being cultivated, and this was generating wealth. As a result, the population was growing because there was more to eat. And artists and merchants and intellectuals began to flourish in unprecedented numbers. Great cities fostered them, and they in turn contributed to the growth of these cities. Merchants became the first members of the middle class. They rapidly rose to power. Standardized currency appeared to facilitate the purchase and sale of merchandise. The men of the Renaissance felt the world could be perfected, that—even if there were outbreaks of plague and war and famine—they could improve things. But first they had to explore the earth. The compass already existed, and the rudder was invented. Soon small ships with enormous sails were ploughing the waves.

A Portuguese caravel from the late 15th century.

The Ponte Vecchio.

It was in the middle of the Renaissance, in 1492, that Christopher Columbus, seeking a western route to India, discovered America.

The most important visual legacy of the Renaissance consists of works of art that have come down to us: buildings, paintings, sculptures, and drawings. They teach us that Renaissance artists were often inspired by antiquity, especially ancient Greece. The culture of the Renaissance encouraged these artists to invent under the sign of clarity.

The capital of beauty, invention, and dreams in 1450 was Florence. Florence—the city of Lorenzo the Magnificent, the city in which Leonardo da Vinci served his apprenticeship and produced his earliest works.

The Palazzo Medici in Florence (1396–1472), designed by the architect Michelozzi Michelozzo.

Leonardo da Vinci was a man of his time, a scientific man who dreamed of a scientific art with a rigor comparable to that of mathematics. He was trying to find new ways for men and women to live in the world. He knew very well that prosperity had changed the relation between man and nature, between man and God, and between man and the powerful.

In this new Renaissance world, with its division of labor, Leonardo would be a complete artist, and also. . . . But I'm forgetting the basics! Let me give them to you without further delay.

Leonardo was born on April 15, 1452 in Vinci, near Florence. He was the son of a man named Piero, a notary, and a peasant woman named Catarina. When Leonardo was born, Johannes Gensfleisch of Mayence, better known as Gutenberg, had just devised the most important invention since gunpowder: the printing press. This was a press with moveable typeface. It was a press that would make possible the publication of 20 million volumes in a 50-year period, from 1450 to 1500. And it was a press that would be one of the rare novelties, one of the rare technical advances, one of the rare tangible achievements of the men of the Renaissance to which Leonardo of Florence would pay but scant attention.

Rosa Rose, I wish you a strong headwind.
Like you, I keep my eye out every day for the postman.

Your uncle Leo

P.S.: Leonardo's word of wisdom for the day, to encourage you to remain curious: "The desire for knowledge comes naturally to those who are good."

The garden of the Palazzo Medici.

General view of Florence.

Dear uncle,
Dear uncle,

No, I'm not stammering. I write "dear uncle" twice because you've already sent me two letters. So: Thank you. Thank you. You tell me Leonardo was one of the greatest of all human geniuses. This confuses me. Is that like the genies in the *Thousand and One Nights*?

I'd also like to know whether this "genius" was ever a child. Was Leonardo ever a screaming baby in this Renaissance, which if you're to be believed was as brilliant and precious as a bouquet of lilacs?

This year, in my garden, the lilacs give off a perfume that's so strong you can hardly believe it!

Drawing by Leonardo representing the valley of the Arno, where he was born. This is the artist's earliest dated work: August 5, 1473.

RosaRosa,

Your word-gardening this spring is quite something. Your last short letter was a veritable alphabetical bouquet.

Today, imagine I'm speaking to you softly, very softly right into your ear. Listen carefully.

Leonardo was indeed a child, even a baby. You needn't have had any doubts about this. He was born in the spring. I've already told you his birth date in numbers, so now I give it to you in letters. He was born on Saturday the fifteenth of April, fourteen hundred fifty-two. He was born in Vinci, a very small village not far from Florence. His mother Catarina was twenty-two and his father Piero twenty-six. Leonardo was an illegitimate child, which means that his father and mother were not married.

Vinci, the village where Leonardo was born.

The year of his birth, his father left for Florence to marry a young, middle-class woman who was 16 at the time. A few months later, his mother Catarina married a very humble man who lived close to Vinci. It's very painful for a baby to have to share its mother. Yes, having a father married to one person and a mother married to another makes for a complicated childhood!

Leonardo would suffer from his illegitimacy until his death. He grew up in Vinci. As an infant he was with his natural mother. He remained with her only until he no longer needed her milk. Afterwards he lived with his grandfather, his father's father. The old Antonio da Vinci had a bit of land from which he made a modest living raising grapes, olives, a little wheat, and a little buckwheat. All these things grew in a landscape of pronounced but rounded hills. In this natural setting,

Leonardo absorbed the smells of the seasons, spoke to the clouds, and even sang—to mingle his voice with that of nature. He observed the flight of birds, and later remembered that "from time to time as I lay in the cradle a vulture came to me and opened my mouth with its tail and struck me many times with its tail inside my lips." He would love birds all his life, the way a child loves the mother's breast that gives it so much happiness and pleasure. It is said that later, when he was a famous painter, he would go to the bird market and, after having paid the stipulated price, open the birds' cages and set them free.

If Leonardo da Vinci hadn't been an illegitimate child, perhaps he would never have been a painter. During this period, illegitimate children had limited options. To take one example: the professional organization of judges and notaries to which Leonardo's father Piero belonged prohibited illegitimate children from membership. Leonardo's choices were limited. So he became a painter.

Piero showed some of his son's drawings to a great artist in Florence, Andrea del Verrocchio. It is said that the older painter marvelled at Leonardo's work. And so it began. At age 14, Leonardo became a student of the great Verrocchio in Florence.

Leonardo was fascinated by all the tools used by the master and his students in creating their works, and took to them quickly. From the start of his apprenticeship, he felt equal to the birds who reinvent clouds by chopping off their peaks. He felt equal to birds whose ability to fly set him dreaming, and superior to the winged creatures tracing patterns against the clear blue sky.

I nearly forgot: the Italian name for the century in which Leonardo was born, the 15th century, is *Quattrocento*. Isn't it a wonderful word? When your legs have healed, you can use it to tightrope walk or play hopscotch:

Quattrocento
Early?
Trocentoqua
Silly?
Centoquattro
Backwards?
Toquattrocen
Almost
Quattrocento!
Quattrocento!

Your uncle Leo

P.S.: Today Leonardo is mischievous enough to pose you a riddle. "Those who have worked the hardest will be the most beaten—their children raised, flayed, and crushed. The answer? Walnut trees whose nuts are knocked down with poles."

Ink drawings of birds' wings, from a manuscript by Leonardo on the flight of birds.

Dear uncle,

I'm still in the garden. The afternoon is over. The heat has faded and the light of the sky has almost disappeared. Where to? Probably the South Pole, to see if the flowers and people there walk upside down.

As you can see, I'm dreaming. Your daily letters encourage my dreams.

I dream with ears, eyes, and mouth open, and my eyes wide open, too.

Your letters make the sky seem bluer. They dress it up. And my latest dream suggests that every day Leonardo rediscovered the sky's wondrous blue and saw himself in it. This blue is so large and yet so light that sometimes I'm afraid it will just float away.

I speak. I speak to myself, and to you. But now it's your turn again. Did Leonardo paint? What did he paint? Tell me about his first work. Was it Mona Lisa's sister? What about Florence?

Rosa

David, a bronze statue realized by Verrocchio toward 1473. Tradition has it Leonardo was the model.

Rosa,

I am a poet but I'm far from sure that I know everything, as you maintain. But my memory is good enough for me to be able to quote you a bit of poetry that I love:

Leonardo da Vinci, deep mirror of darkness,
Where angels appear, their smiles charged with
mystery
And tenderness, within the shadowy enclosures
Of pines and glaciers that shut in their country.

These lines are by Charles Baudelaire. Chew them like gum to be sure you've learned them by heart. I cite them because Leonardo's first painting was already an angel, one in a large work executed in the Verrocchio studio, *The Baptism of Christ.*

Behind this angel is a landscape with rocks and sheer cliffs. Despite the palm tree, it's not hard to imagine pines punctuating the foreground and a glacier meeting the sky at the horizon.

Verrocchio, *The Baptism of Christ*, detail. The left angel is said to have been painted by Leonardo.

This angel present at Christ's baptism already has the smiling sweetness that would characterize Leonardo's later faces. Part of its mystery derives from the fact that we only see it in three-quarter view from the back.

Admire this face that wants to be the focus of every eye. Admire this gaze that resembles a caress.

Leonardo was 20 years old when he painted this angel, in the *bottega* of his master Andrea di Michele di Francesco de Cioni, known as Andrea del Verrocchio. Bottega is the Italian word for workshop. Leonardo was only an apprentice when he first entered Verrocchio's service. He would subsequently become a fellow workman and then a master. The process was prolonged and exacting. Everyone working in the bottega obeyed the master and respected him. They all lived there along with the master's family. Before becoming one of these manipulators of forms and colors we now call artists, the student assistants cleaned brushes and tools, did shopping, lit and looked after the fire, cooked the varnishes and sizing gum, ground paints, and prepared the supports—if not canvas, then linden wood or willow. During all this time they drew and drew, imitating their master. They worked as a team. The Verrocchio bottega, where important artists such as Perugino, Lorenzo di Credi, and even Botticelli spent time, was a breeding ground for new ideas and new talents. It was a laboratory in which students sharpened their critical intelligence and experimented. Innovation was valued there. In Verrocchio's studio, invention was the norm.

Verrocchio, *The Baptism of Christ* (1472–1475).

When he became an apprentice at age 14, Leonardo knew how to read, write, and work with figures. In other words, he didn't know very much. Verrocchio's studio would be his university, as would the city of Florence generally. It was here that he became a draftsman, a painter, a geometer, an architect, a goldsmith, a metalworker, a mechanic—and that's not all. At age 20, he achieved the status of master, like his teacher, whom he soon equaled and even surpassed in skill. He would always cherish the memory of having executed, under his guidance, a metal sphere almost 20 feet in diameter.

A sphere weighing almost two tons, hoisted to a height of 352 feet to the top of the Cathedral of Saint Maria of the Flowers. Rosa-of-the-flowers, you must one day go and see this dome by the architect Brunelleschi. When you do, you'll be able to sense what the surrounding city was like in the Renaissance, with its dozens of studios for working wood, marble, and metal. Florence is the city through which the Arno flows, laughing as it passes beneath the Ponte Vecchio (when it isn't flooding). It is also the city of flowers in which old neighborhoods give way to beautiful palazzi with hidden interior courts, formidable structures that turn away from light and sun alike. The city and its streets are an education for the eye. There all is linear purity, spatial clarity, elegant masonry, and handsome symmetry. A prosperous metropolis where coins (called florins) were minted, Florence boasted more than 100,000 inhabitants and dominated Tuscany. It was in Florence that Leonardo, at the age of 20, painted the angel in the *Baptism of Christ*. Only 20, and he was already a master!

Leonardo knew everything he needed to know about his art. He was already at ease with the oil paints from Flanders, which made possible a new luminosity and brilliance, allowing for unprecedented control of tonal gradations.

Drawing. Presumed self-portrait of Leonardo from about 1512.

He is 20
He is beautiful
He has a lovely voice
He can be both grave and playful
He wears pink and likes jewels
He loves rich linen and silk fabrics from Flanders, the Levant, and
    Cyprus.
He is 20
He's become capable of inventing himself.
He knows he can shape the future, generating life and happiness
    like nature. And he could already have written, in his left-
    handed script: "The painter is the rival of nature."

Your uncle Leo

P.S.: I quoted Baudelaire at the beginning of this letter. Leonardo said: "Anyone . . . who invokes authors is using not his intellect but his memory."
P.P.S.: Verrocchio was a very great artist and beloved of Leonardo. One day, in one of his notebooks, Leonardo wrote: "Unfortunate is the student who never surpasses his master."

The Cathedral of Florence, dedicated to Saint Mary of the Flowers (Santa Maria dei Fiori).

Rosa,

I magine: I've just spent the night in Florence in a dream. I was with Leonardo! We met at the church of San Lorenzo. Leonardo was handsome this night, as he is every day and every night. His long hair gave him an air of frivolity, but he spoke to me with great seriousness. With him, everything is double. I've seen him write backwards with his left hand. His writing set me dreaming within my dream, making me think of mirrors that consume time—which never stops slipping through Leonardo's fingers. The passage of time tends to wipe away the traces even of Leonardo, as of many others. It has seen works damaged or destroyed altogether.

Leonardo spoke to me softly as we walked, and all at once we saw windows decked out with olive branches. We heard trumpet calls piercing the air. The bells not only of the cathedral but of all the city's churches rang out. Games were beginning on the piazza. Horses galloped, pulling chariots dressed with garlands; the colored banners of wealthy horsemen flapped in the wind. The celebration concluded, Leonardo showed me several of his early works in his studio. His young assistants surrounded him. Some of his friends were there—philosophers, doctors, and mathematicians. He showed all of us his *Annunciation* and his *Madonna with Child*, and also his magnificent portrait of the beautiful *Ginevra di Benci*.

I listened to him. I was seduced by so much beauty. Each of these paintings made clear the subtlety of Leonardo's handling of oils: so subtle that one might think his brushes were as fine as a single strand of hair. Sometimes, things are more easily understood in dreams. In this case, I grasped that for Leonardo the mere reproduction of appearances, however accomplished, was never enough.

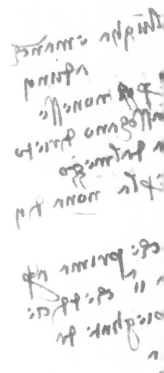

Madonna (1478–1480).

Painting must have a soul. It is this soul that holds our gaze. Rosa, I'm going to tell you what words come to me as I examine these youthful works by Leonardo. Look at the *Annunciation*. Its setting prefigures those of the *Saint Anne* and the *Mona Lisa*.

It is this composition in depth, very carefully painted, that fixes the painting in our minds. It envelopes the whole in a remarkable unity.

Look at the beautiful *Ginevra di Benci*. The mature Leonardo is already present here. The light has an enigmatic quality. In the background we see part of the landscape in which Leonardo grew up—the part without forbidding rocks. Art encourages artists to reflect on their own pasts. Here Leonardo, who like every adult retained memories of his childhood, offers us a vision of childhood that has been purified by his brush. Ginevra is beautiful. She captivates us. Is she about to speak? It might seem so. But no: the painting is mute. We others, spectators of its beauty, see in the painting something so dense that we sense a source within it, a source of life and love that could flow like the mother's milk believed by the child to be eternal.

Portrait of *Ginevra di Benci* (1474–1476).

The Annunciation (1472–1475) (Oil on wood.)

Leonardo had very sharp eyes. It's as though he always saw more and more clearly than others. It was thanks to his eye that his brush found its accord with nature. It enabled him to instill his receding landscapes and his figures with a simple, original beauty. Allow your gaze to linger. Leonardo's painting is never smugly triumphant. On the contrary, it is always quite restrained. As for myself, I like Ginevra's unforced, natural quality. When I look at her, I see a young contemporary woman about to smile and sing for me. In Leonardo's world, beauty and love are inseparable from everyday life, like the divine mystery. Look at his *Madonna with Child*. Here the Virgin Mary is just a woman like any other. As a result, she becomes all the more beautiful, all the more exemplary. She's playing with her child. Here, Leonardo demonstrates, as he would later do in his extraordinary *Virgin of the Rocks* and *Saint Anne*, that the happy, fragile love of a mother is the truest love.

It was good to dream about Florence last night, to dream about it for you. Like every artist I encountered there—Donatello, Uccello, Verrocchio, Botticelli, Ghirlandaio, Michelangelo—when I awoke this morning I sensed I'd been stamped by the city's imprint.

Your uncle Leo

P.S.: Leonardo's riddle for the day: "What is it that men ardently desire but are unaware of once they have it?" Answer: "Sleep."

Study of drapery (brush, bistre, with white highlights, on canvas.)

My dear uncle,

*I*n your last letter, you spoke about your dream as though you'd woken up in order to look at yourself in your dream. You speak to me, you write to me, and I dream about you. I dream about you in the company of Leonardo. Two Leos in Florence! Two Leos in Verrocchio's studio! And what now? Do we stay in Florence? Or do we move on to Venice, Padua, Bologna, Verona, Ravenna, Ferrara, or Milan?

I don't know these cities, but dictionaries talk when you open them up, and these names jump off the page. In the middle of the pages on Tuscany, I encountered a certain Col-

lodi who was helping out Pinocchio, but that section was about another period. So?

Do we travel or not?
Do you write me everything?
What will you write me?
Find babbling words for me like the flame of a candle, words that will squeeze me in their arms!

Rosa

Rosa,

Let's travel, since you want to and since Leonardo left Florence. At age 30, he arrived in Milan. While Florence boasted pure lines composing beautiful perspectives, Milan was much messier. As a city it was jumbled and irregular, but it was a sociable place whose inhabitants liked to eat and converse. It was talkative, like the flamboyant Gothic style of its churches.

Leonardo settled in Milan. He remained there for 17 years. In 1483, he painted his first great masterpiece, *The Virgin of the Rocks*. It was commissioned by the superiors of the Confraternity of the Conception. Don't forget that in this period all works were executed for specific commissions. The contract between artist and patron stipulated everything about the painting: format, medium, subject, number of figures, their general arrangement in the painting, and even the colors to be used. When he started painting this work, Leonardo knew he would violate the conditions of the contract. He would paint in his own way, trusting his own judgment. He would be not only a master, but his own master. The completed work was so different from what had been stipulated by the confraternity that the matter went to litigation in a trial that lasted 20 years. But the painting's beauty, seductiveness, and originality astonished the Milanese.

The Virgin of the Rocks, detail.

In this painting, Leonardo shows us the Virgin in front of a grotto. An angle is with her, as are two children who are Jesus and Saint John. But the real subject of the painting as realized by Leonardo is light. *The Virgin of the Rocks* is dominated by *chiaroscuro,* or the play of light and dark. Look carefully: one, two, three . . . and you're at the theater. Examine the painted light that creates volume here, rather like the lighting on our stages today. If nature and the human figures constitute a unity and are at peace with one another in front of this grotto, that's because everything is enveloped in the same light. The technique of *chiaroscuro,* with its subtle gradations between darkness and light, eliminates the doubt separating man from nature. With his self-knowledge, the Renaissance man can familiarize himself with nature and conquer his fears. The especially delicate light here, known in Italian as *sfumato,* creates an atmosphere in which the bodies and faces seem to emerge from a dark sea. In this fusion of man and nature, God's power was somewhat diminished. Take a closer look. In the background, the receding grotto is like the beginning of an eternal tunnel, an eternal fear. But a mysterious light keeps watch. This grotto is suggestive of the forbidding landscape around Vinci. It's as though Leonardo had found his childhood memories to be the most fruitful source for forms and volumes. It's also interesting, when we remember the circumstances of Leonardo's childhood, that the infant Jesus here is fatherless. And that he has a mother of astonishing beauty.

The Virgin of the Rocks (1483–1486).

The Virgin of the Rocks,
details.

In this work, there's not a single space, a single volume, a single face that isn't carefully defined in terms of light and dark. The visual unity is accentuated by an effect of transparency. It is this quality that dominates the whole. The tranparency of the colors (examine the sleeves) is so remarkable because Leonardo superimposed several thin layers of oil paint. It really is as though we were at the theater. Everything is designed to glorify the soft light, and the angel looks at us with complicity. The blue of the Virgin's mantle and the red of the angel's garment speak to one another and are united by means of the green that intervenes between them. Leonardo established another reality. He transformed the simple biblical story he was supposed to depict.

There's no gold leaf, nothing dazzling or showy.

The rounded forms of the hands and faces summon the spectator towards them. Never has a painter devised a composition with so much to offer the eye.

The lesson taught
by Leonardo's light is
so compelling that it would
be admired and absorbed by
painters as different as Rembrandt,
Caravaggio, and Georges de la Tour.

I love this Madonna so vividly present in front of a grotto. I look at her and say to myself that perhaps Leonardo, in painting her, thought that men might obtain an infinite earthly power if only they could gain access to more love—that painting, a human art, might be able to increase the amount of love available to mankind.

Rosa, it's a beautiful day. Enjoy it as best you can.

Your uncle Leo

P.S.: Art is never naive. It is never the result of chance. Reflect on this observation by Leonardo: "The painter who works using his skill and the judgment of his eyes but without consulting his reason is like a mirror that reflects all the objects in front of it without knowing them."

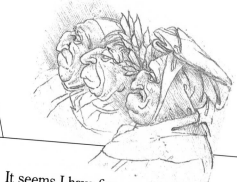

Dear uncle Leo,

After opening your last letter, I read it and reread it.
Then I read it out loud so that all the light in the garden could enjoy it. I even sang some of the words.

Keep talking to me about painting—about all its aspects. Don't just offer me cheese and dessert, I want something heartier, something like a main course. I have so many questions. Was Leonardo married? What did he do when he wasn't painting? I know I'm always doing something, even when I'm doing nothing. I talk to myself inside my head, or listen to the perfume of the flowers, or breathe in the noises around me.

It seems I have five senses like everybody else, but they're not enough for me. So I mix them up.
The lilacs in the garden are fading.
Yesterday the rain fell without making a sound.
This morning there's a new daffodil, proud but delicate.
I'd like to give it to you.
I'd also like to give it to Leonardo.
I always like things that are impossible.

Rosa

P.S.: Recommend a book, a novel, that's set in Leonardo's time.

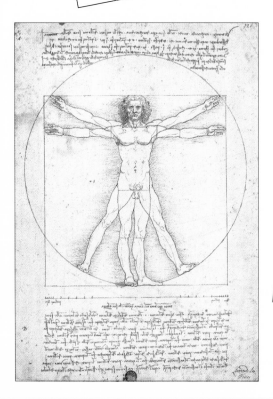

Schema of human bodily proportions, with notes in Leonardo's hand (about 1492).

Rosa,

Read and listen to everything I write you today with your eyes, your ears, your hands (both of them), your nose, the tip of your tongue, your toes, your knees, and each of your thousands of strands of hair.

Leonardo was above all a painter. He tells us that the 10 considerations crucial to a painter's work are: light, shadow, color, volume, figure, placement, distance, proximity, movement, and rest. For him, painting was not solely a matter of manual dexterity but also a thing of the mind.

He was a painter, but he also acquired remarkable expertise in geology, optics, acoustics, mathematics, anatomy, hydraulics, balistics, naval armaments, botany, and gravitation. His notebooks reveal that he was also a philosopher. He was the Renaissance man writ large, and everything in his life was oriented towards his intellectual emancipation. His versatility was astonishing, and the sweet exaltation of his being, like that of his painting, was rooted in his profound commitment to enlightenment. This commitment was never solely a matter of knowledge. He said that "the painter is the rival of nature." For his part, he established a rivalry between his own life and that surrounding him— in other words, with the customs, norms, and ideas of his time.

Caricatures and grotesque heads (about 1490).

Yes, Leonardo was an intuitive person who speculated and then experimented.

Like all creative individuals, he was sceptical about the values that prevailed in the world around him. He was curious and rigorous, and transcended conventional categories. His painting was fearless, like he himself. Again, both he and his painting managed to get beyond the fears inhibiting the people of his age. Leonardo was a maverick in both his life and his work, in everything he touched.

We must never forget that the Renaissance painters who created so many marvels were regarded as the servants of princes, of the rich. Most often, their official status was no better than that of grooms, and at the French royal court they were the equals of valets! Through his conduct, Leonardo challenged the acceptability of obliging artists to constantly humiliate themselves by bowing and scraping to the rich and powerful, to princes and religious officials. Painters waited for commissions awarded by their patrons, and sometimes the wait was long indeed! These patrons did not act out of pure love for art, but rather in view of having some of art's prestige reflect back on themselves. Artists were not always paid for their work, and even when they were it was often only after lengthy delays. It was to the patron's advantage to keep them wanting, like beggars.

Vasari, who was the first biographer of Leonardo and many other Renaissance masters, wrote: "When more energy must be expended in obtaining food than in cultivating renown, unhappy genius remains in obscurity and never becomes known (through the shameful pride of those capable of helping him but who can't be bothered)."

Leonardo dressed and behaved as though he were royalty.

He did exactly what he liked.

Isabella d'Este of Mantua was a great patron of the arts, the elder sister of the deceased Beatrice d'Este and thus the sister-in-law of Lodovico il Moro. The powerful Isabella d'Este found in Leonardo da Vinci a painter who resisted her will, going so far as to leave Mantua for Venice rather than staying to serve her! He was the only painter of the era who never allowed anyone to capture him. Isabella d'Este obtained commissions from and dealt high-handedly with Botticelli, Perugino, Mantegna, Titian, and Raphael—but not Leonardo.

He was something of a rebel. He was wary of inspiration. He created an art born of work and reflection, in which reason figured prominently. And in this respect, he was remarkably modern. In each of his works, he displayed his knowledge of the world as well as his beliefs, which differed considerably from those held dear by his patrons.

He wasn't a prophet, just a painter.

He wasn't superhuman, just a man using his reason—a man deeply opposed to superstition and suspicious of compliments.

Raphael, *Madonna of the Baldachino.*

Rosa, when you feel strong emotions while looking at Leonardo's paintings, bear in mind that artists evoking such responses in their viewers, readers, or listeners must often isolate themselves from the world to achieve these results.

Artists can be regarded as geniuses or as delinquents. There have been times in the past when the two words were more or less interchangeable.

Geniuses? Delinquents?

They don't respect tradition. They invent. They have one eye on the present and another on the future.

Leonardo eyed the future lovingly, intent upon blending it into his works.

In his own century, he maintained that painters should be regarded as intellectuals rather than craftsmen. He held that painting should be classed among the liberal arts along with poetry and music, not with the mechanical arts like gilding and saddlery.

In my next letter I'll tell you about larger projects undertaken by Leonardo, about transformations and technical innovations foreseen by him. Today I've spoken about the man in his century, in the world. A man whose beauty and dignity were as provocative as the softness and grace of his paintings. He never married. Most of the time he was surrounded by boys or young men who were his students. The distance he kept from the girls and women he painted so lovingly makes me think of a phrase by the poet Petrarch, quoted by Vasari when discussing Leonardo's failure to complete many of his projects: "the work was delayed by desire." Rosa, Leonardo was deprived of his mother at such an early age, and he powerfully evoked her along with the rest of the world's women—soft, smiling, enigmatic—in his creations.

Rosa, while waiting for my next words
let yourself go, open up
let painting inside you
leave it there
it will enrich you

Your uncle Leo

P.S.: Don't forget what Leonardo said: "Man is the model of the world."

Woman with an Ermine
(1483–1490).

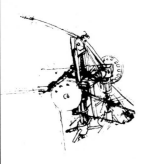

Rosa,

Milan, where Leonardo lived from 1482, was ruled by Ludovico Sforza, more often called Ludovico il Moro.

Leonardo worked in several capacities for this prince and the Milanese. This was the period of his full maturity. He was the perfect painter-sculptor-goldsmith-designer. He was also a technician, a scientist, and a philosopher who described and sketched his ideas and projects.

Leonardo was a universal man, an inventor who—incredible as it may seem—described and sketched dream textile machines, flying machines, parachutes, bridges, interlocking spiral staircases, canals, levee systems, even contact lenses for those with bad vision. He was sure of himself and his prescience in numerous domains to the point of audacity. Here is a letter he wrote to Ludovico Sforza, enumerating for his patron the skills of the artist-engineer who was Leonardo the Florentine:

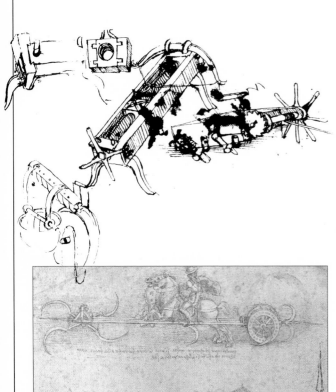

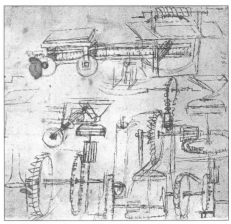

Studies of hydraulic machines. Left, two of Leonardo's most interesting machines of war: a chariot outfitted with turning scythes and a blind chariot operable by hand or horsepower.

Most Illustrious Lord, having already sufficiently considered the experiments of those who pretend to be great inventors of war machines, and having observed that the aforesaid machines differ in no salient respects from those commonly employed, I feel obliged, without intending injury to anyone, to reveal my secrets to Your Excellence, to whom I propose to execute, at his convenience, all the things briefly described below.

1. I have a model for bridges that are very solid and light, extremely easy to transport, thanks to which you could pursue or, if need be, flee the enemy; and for others that are robust and resistant to fire as well as assaults that are easy to build and dismantle. I also know how to go about burning and destroying those of the enemy.

2. For sieges, I know how to dry up the water in moats and construct an infinite number of bridges, battering rams, scaling ladders, and other machines intended to assist in such enterprises.

3. Item. If, due to the height of embankments or the strength of a position, it is impossible to subdue this position by bombardment, I know of methods whereby any citadel or fortress that's not built on rock could be destroyed, etc.

4. I also have models of very practical and easily transportable mortars with which I can deliver so many small stones it will almost seem to be raining, the smoke from which will instill terror in the enemy, sowing harm and confusion among them.

5. Item. I know how, by tortuous and secret passages and tunnels excavated without noise, to reach a desired goal, even if it is necessary to pass beneath a moat or a river.

6. Item. I will make vehicles that are covered, reliable, and indestructible, and that, penetrating the enemy ranks with their artillery, will destroy the most powerful force; the infantry can follow after them without encountering obstacles or suffering harm.

7. Item. Should the need arise, I will make large bombards, mortars, and fire engines in beautiful and useful forms, different from those now in use.

8. Should bombardment fail, I will make catapults, mangonels, trabocchi, and other unusual and marvelously effective machines. In short, according to need, I can invent various and infinite machines for attack as well as defense.

9. And if the encounter should take place at sea, I have numerous very efficient machines for attack as well as defense; and ships resistant to the discharge of the largest canon, whether powder or steam.

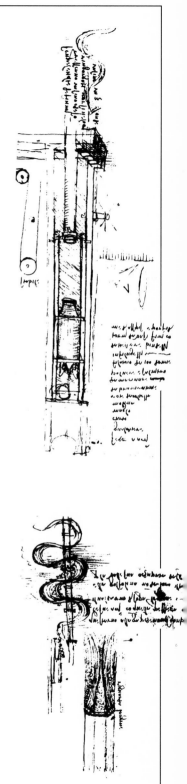

Study for the Sforza monument (facsimile).

10. In peacetime, I believe myself capable of giving perfect satisfaction and anyone's equal in the matter of architecture, in the composition of public and private buildings, and in the transport of water from one place to another.

Item. I can execute sculpture in marble, bronze, or clay; and in painting make works of absolutely any kind as well as anyone, whoever he might be.

In addition, a bronze horse could also be executed that would be to the immortal glory and eternal honor of the Honorable lord your father, of happy memory, and the illustrious house of Sforza.

And if any of the things mentioned above should strike some as being impossible or unrealizable, I am prepared to test them in your park or any other place agreeable to Your Excellency—to whom I recommend myself in all humility.

The Most Illustrious Lord commissioned Leonardo to make the bronze horse mentioned in the letter. On it, Leonardo was to place a figure of Ludovico's father, Duke Francesco, armed for battle.

Leonardo executed a clay model that was exhibited in 1493, on the occasion of the announcement of the engagement of Bianca Maria Sforza, the Moor's illegitimate daughter. The Milanese were astonished. Everyone felt that nothing so sublime had been achieved since antiquity.

By the time Leonardo showed his horse, he had accrued enormous prestige and everyone in the city was aware of his brilliance. Vasari wrote of this horse: "Those who saw the large model he executed in clay maintain they never saw a more beautiful work, or one more impressive." It remained in place in Milan until the arrival of the French, who smashed it into pieces.

The *gran-cavallo* was never cast, and in 1494 the 72 tons of bronze intended for the project were made into canons needed for the war.

The Milanese period was not exclusively preoccupied with war, far from it. There were marriages, births, baptisms, and meetings between princes, all of which were occasions for theatrical perform- ances, games, juggling, and poetry. Leonardo, whose inventive capacities were prodigious, made sure the festivities dazzled and entertained. As conceiver, designer, and director, he created worlds in which the dozens of powerful guests at these events could move about joyfully and happily. His contemporaries were particularly taken with a ball of the planets organized in January of 1490, speaking of the delights and surprises he devised for it as so many marvels.

Studies of horses.

But while Leonardo was equal to any creative challenge, he was above all a painter, and in Milan he realized a work that would be enormously influential, closing the door on one style and opening it wide to another.

Rosa, if I've given you a mouthful about painting and prompted you yourself to talk about it, that makes me very happy. Now it will be that much easier for you to paint your own life and dreams.

Your uncle Leo

P.S.: Don't put too much confidence in your dreams, even if they're dressed up in rainbow colors. Our Leo thought that "the imagination doesn't see as clearly as the eye."

My dearest uncle,

I spent part of the night at the window. I looked at the garden's jumble of flowers and leaves. It was clear and the moon was almost full.

All the same, the night was dark. Does night have the power not to be dark?

Does night have the power not to obscure the garden's laughing daylight face?

In the middle of the night, I noticed a different kind of silence. It was as though the absence of manmade noise made time and space contract a bit. As I listened, I wouldn't have been too surprised to hear the gallop of Leonardo's horse.

Last night the words of your letters were like so many night butterflies dancing with the stars. I'm anxious to be healed, to dance a bit myself. So many of the words you've given me might serve as my partners, my escorts into another domain—perhaps on horseback. Now I know about Leonardo's great horse. Tell me what happened next.

Tell me about the masterpiece you mentioned. Tell me about the next exploit of Leonardo the Florentine—of Milan.

I eagerly await the arrival of the postman each day.

Rosa

The Last Supper (1495–1497).

Rose,

I think I understand how you've come to be on such intimate terms with the flowers in your garden. Doubtless you speak softly to them and they answer in a language of flowers that only you can understand. I imagine you seated, your legs encased in plaster. You are calm and nature is laughing all around you. But close your eyes. Try to put the smiling blooms out of your mind and return to Milan at the end of the *Quattrocento*.

About 1495, Ludovico commissioned Leonardo to execute a mural painting for the refectory of the convent of Santa Maria delle Grazie.

Leonardo produced a monumental religious painting, a Last Supper. He chose to depict a dramatic moment in Christ's last meal with his disciples. In Leonardo's *Last Supper*, the actual meal is already over, though bread and wine are still scattered over the table. Leonardo represented the precise moment in which Christ announces, or rather the moment immediately after he has announced, that someone at the table would betray him. He has just said: "The one who will betray me is here," and "Verily I say unto you, one of you will betray me." Look carefully.

Look at this work which time has ravaged, and of which one art historian has said, "His great *Last Supper*—in which an inner drama sends ripples in every direction, twisting and sculpting human forms like trees bending before a hurricane—offers the greatest study of psychological dynamics in all of painting." Note the calm figure of Christ in the center of this storm, and the figures of, from left to right: Bartholomew, James the Minor, Andrew, Judas, Peter, John, Thomas, James the Major, Phillip, Matthew, Thadeus, and Simon. In this work Leonardo demonstrates the extent of his involvement with real life— with its tragedies, its glories, and its betrayals. In executing it, he didn't sprint toward completion like Giotto when realizing a fresco. No: he proceeded step by step, face by face, finger by finger. Here he performed as a master painter turned choreographer. Look at the dance played out among the hands alone. They are so characterized that each of them infers a specific assertion or question. If we could see nothing but these hands, we would still have a ballet of bird-like forms in space: a ballet shaped with remarkable skill, intelligence, and psychological penetration.

Leonardo, who sought out models in churches, public baths, taverns, and markets as well as in the street and prison, needed much time to perfect the work.

His eye was like a predator, stalking all Milan to find the bodies and faces he needed.

The Last Supper, detail.

Study for *The Last Supper*, details.

Here's what Vasari had to say about the *Last Supper*: "What Leonardo set out to express was the anxious concern of the apostles, their desire to know who would betray their master. Their faces show love, fear, indignation, and bewilderment provoked by their inability to grasp Christ's full meaning. Just as striking is the resolve, hatred, and treachery of Judas. Even the smallest parts of the work are treated with astonishing exactitude. The very weave of the tablecloth is painted such that one would take it for real linen. The story goes that the prior was in a great hurry to have the work finished. It seemed strange to him that Leonardo sometimes spent half a day in front of it, lost in reflection. He would have had him work continuously like the laborers digging in his garden, never putting down his brush. He even complained to the duke and asked that he summon Leonardo. By the adroit way in which he requested that the work be finished, the duke made clear his embarrassment at the prior's insistence. Knowing the prince's intelligence and tact, Leonardo explained himself at length, which he'd never done to the prior. He spoke of art and pointed out that elevated minds often work hardest when they seem to be doing the least; at such moments they are exploring the unfamiliar and seeking

The Last Supper, details.   the perfect form for ideas they subsequently express by using their

hands to shape things previously conceived in their minds. He added that only two heads remained to be done: that of Christ, the likeness of which he could not hope to find on earth and had not yet been able to create in his imagination with the beauty and grace required for an image of God incarnate; and that of Judas, which was giving him much trouble, for he felt incapable of imagining the facial expression of someone who, after having received so many benefits from him, had a soul so black as to betray our Lord, the Creator of the world. He would keep looking, however, and if he found nothing better, he could always use the head of the prior, who was so troublesome and indiscreet. The duke laughed heartily at this and asserted he was absolutely right. The poor bewildered prior turned his attention to his garden, letting Leonardo finish the head of Judas in peace, and it is indeed the very image of treachery and wickedness." I point out Christ's red robe (red: color of the passion) and the rhythms of the composition, which seem to unfold in waltz time: three apostles, three apostles, Christ, three apostles, three apostles. But I leave it to you to decipher the facial expressions.

For once, this is a work that doesn't bring to mind the circumstances of Leonardo's birth and childhood. There's no landscape suggestive of Vinci, nor is there one of Leonardo's haunting mother-virgin figures. Having expended considerable effort to explore the connections between art and nature, he here confounds the two. Paradoxically and despite himself, by setting Christ so calmly apart he devised an image of the contrast between the turbulence, anxiety, and disorder prevailing on earth and the peace of the life to come.

Rosa, tomorrow I'll write a bit more about the *Last Supper* and the science of perspective.

Uncle Leo

P.S.: The range of character depicted in this *Last Supper* makes me think of the following remark by Leonardo: "Speaking well of an unworthy man is every bit as wrong as speaking ill of a virtuous man."

Rosa,

Try to envision it: Leonardo is about seven feet above the ground on his scaffolding. It's early in the morning but it's already hot. Perhaps it's early summer. The *Last Supper* is almost finished. His students are there. All is calm. Yesterday there were several intense two-hour painting sessions interrupted by breaks for reflection.

Today he just looks and remains silent. All those who've come to see the almost-completed work are astonished.

Leonardo is still dissatisfied.

He assesses the organization of the artificial theater he has devised. He imagines invisible perspective lines shaping the painting's space.

Perspective is the art of making a flat plane seem to recede into depth. It is one of the means developed in the West to make art seem more real than real.

It is a way of creating the illusion that painted objects are enveloped in three-dimensional space, and is largely dependent on their being situated at the proper "distance" from the observing eye. The organizing point of a perspective construction, known as its vanishing point, falls where an imaginary line emanating from the eye intersects with its horizon line. In the *Last Supper,* this vanishing point coincides with the head of Christ. All the painting's receding lines pass through his head! Perspective is capable of powerful effects, yet there remains something theatrical about it, something that must have appealed to Leonardo—who, as we've seen, was both a scientist and a man of the stage.

In this remarkable work, Leonardo calculated his perspective so it would seem a continuation of the room in which it was placed. The spectators seem to inhabit the same space as the drama's participants. So successful is the illusion conjured up by Leonardo's mastery that we, too, seem to be present as it unfolds. We can all the more easily imagine ourselves as the traitor or as one of the faithful disciples figuring in its dynamic of doubt and bewilderment. There is a complex, contradictory interaction between our own point of view, which seems to be the organizing principle of the whole, and the apparently independent life observable within the painting.

Perspective schema of
The Last Supper.

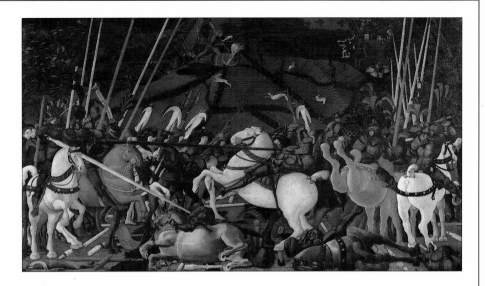

We spectator-participants are still more astonished when we notice that the perspective effect continues beyond the room's back wall, into an atmospheric landscape visible through its three openings.

Most of Leonardo's success here was due to his own considerable gifts and accomplishments, but he was also indebted to the work of his mathematician friend Luca Pacioli, whose important book *De Divina Proportione* would be published some years later, in 1509.

The grave Giotto would have been amazed by the amplitude and openess of this *Last Supper,* and doubtless Paolo Uccello would have been able to make the combatants in his *Battle of San Romano* seem less spatially constricted if he'd painted it after Leonardo's work.

It was done.

Leonardo, who has often been reproached for failing to complete so many of his projects, had achieved the most fully realized painting in the history of art.

Your uncle Leo

P.S.: Leonardo wrote: "Among equal things the one most distant will seem to be the smaller; and its reduction in size will correspond to the extent of its distance." He also wrote: "Treat colors in perspective in a way consistent with the object's dimensions, which is to say such that the colors lose something of their intensity to an extent proportionate with the body's reduction of its natural size."

Rosa,

Have you been devouring this *Last Supper* with your eyes? Have you felt its dramatic intensity? The figures within it are motionless, frozen. They have just heard Christ pronounce a difficult truth. In a flash, a tragic pall has been cast over this happy meal. Leonardo chose to paint the apostles' fright in this terrible moment. It's as though they've been struck by lightning. We see a group of friends undone, the bonds between them snapped. Each of them is preoccupied by his own uneasiness, his own sense of love having suddenly been withdrawn. We are presented with a veritable cataclysm. The harmony prevailing in this small community has been dissolved, it is no longer held together by love's unifying power, and the Christ here is utterly alone—solitary and beautiful. He seems to have crossed a threshold, the one separating life from the beyond. This distant elsewhere toward which Christ already feels himself being drawn finds a visual echo in the placement of his head precisely in front of the vanishing point. His downcast gaze is directed abstractedly into space, but there's no denying its power over us. Today and always, those who believe in the afterlife can find in this face reason for hope.

Leonardo painted a nightmare, for this depiction of the eucharist announces the coming death of Christ with more immediacy than any that had been painted before. It is a palpable presence, just like the light. The supreme mastery of perspective here on both technical and philosophical levels—it seems imbued with both earthly and celestial qualities—sets this work apart as marking the end of one era and the beginning of another.

So remarkable was this depiction of individuals racked by doubt—prompted by the painful revelation that the love of God and his only begotten son were insufficient to spare mankind from betrayal and death—that it launched the visual arts in a new direction.

Your uncle Leo

P.S.: Leonardo wrote the following phrase for himself, but it could well have been uttered by his figure of Christ: "All the while I thought I was learning to live I was in fact learning to die."

Study for *The Last Supper*.

The Last Supper, detail.

My uncle,

*T*he days are getting longer and longer; they're stretching out like rubber. Myself, by both day and night I navigate, I wander, I emigrate, I explore—in short, I travel to the four corners of the globe. From my garden and not school, for I still haven't returned to my classes.

Thanks for telling me about perspective and *The Last Supper.*

Now it's my turn. I've been rummaging through the house (as best I can with my casts) in search of traces of the Renaissance. Not literally: I know that our house isn't an old monastary. I've been looking through books and magazines, and listening to recordings. I've found a few images, but above all some POETRY. So pay attention. For your pleasure, I send you a few lines by poets who lived more or less in Leonardo's time, like Charles d'Orléans, who died in 1465 (when Leonardo was thirteen); and to begin (surprise!), some poems written and set to music by the composer Josquin des Prés. I've just listened to a recording: two voices with lute, and two voices with viols. Try to imagine the music as you read.

LANGUISHING HEART

Languishing heart, beset by sighs,
Pleas, tears, and painful longing,
Be joyful, for your beautiful mistress
Takes pity and wants
to comfort you
With joy, pleasure, and merriment.

TAKE LEAVE

In parting take my love with you,
Don't hold the break against me.
Even those swimming in the sea
Have not suffered greater pain,
For while I find love always bitter
Renunciation of all love-laden looks
Is like a knife-thrust into my heart,
So take leave before it's too late.

Josquin des Pres

Did you know that Josquin des Prés met Leonardo in Milan?

Now, my poet-uncle, read the next one, which made me think of you especially. Perhaps you already know it by heart.

Winter, you are a villain,
Summer is pleasant and kind,
As shown by May and April,
Who never leave its side.

Summer dresses fields and woods
In its livery of green
And countless other colors,
Such that Nature brilliant seems.

But Winter, you bring forth
But snow, wind, rain, and hail;
Exile should be your lot.
Speaking plainly, without guile,
Winter, you are vile.

Charles d'Orléans

I hope you like these lines as much as I do.

It's late afternoon. The shadows have softened. They've gotten longer; perhaps they're straining to reach the vanishing point on the horizon!

Now it's almost dark.

Rosa

P.S.: I'm going to buy myself a sketch-book and draw in the garden and the house—and I'll draw my 10 toes, too, who are now quite anxious to be released from their prison.

Rosa,

Thank you for the poems. The ones by Josquin were new to me, and very beautiful they are, too.

Leonardo the Florentine eventually had to return to Florence. Having returned, he was asked to undertake an immense work there, the most important commission he had yet received. He was to paint a wall of the Great Council Chamber, also known as the Hall of the Five Hundred, in the Palazzo Vecchio.

He decided to represent *The Battle of Anghiari* on this wall; but while he made many preparatory studies for the project and began to execute it, he never brought it to completion.

Presumed studies for *The Battle of Anghiari*. *Skirmish between Cavalry and Foot Soldiers*.

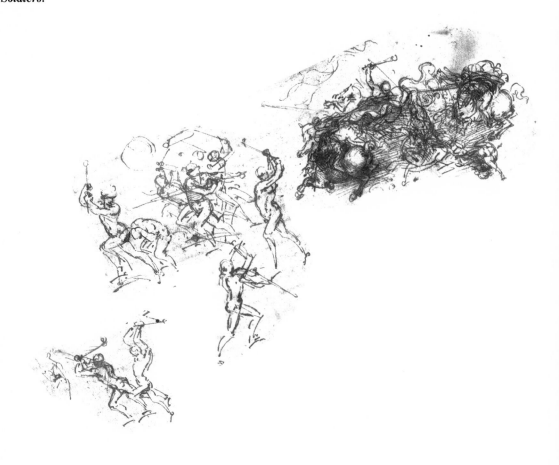

Executed using a novel fresco technique that proved unstable, Leonardo's *Battle of Anghiari* deteriorated rapidly. This is from an anonymous 16th-century copy. (In this period, artists often copied the work of master artists to learn their craft.)

This is what Vasari wrote about the cartoon for this composition: "Fury, hatred, and rage can be read not only in the men but in the horses as well; two of them, front legs interlocked, attack one another with their teeth as violently as their riders in a struggle for the standard. One soldier who has seized it with both hands twists around violently while urging his horse to withdraw, holding fast to it in order to wrench it away from four men surrounding it. Two of the defenders grasp it with one hand while lifting their others to cut the wood with their swords. An old soldier in a red cap grips the standard in one hand while screaming and brandishes a sabre in the other, in a furious attempt to cut off the hands of the two combatants fighting desperately and gritting their teeth in their attempt to defend their flag. Beneath the horses' legs, two soldiers seen in foreshortening engage in combat; one of them, on the ground, thrashes his arms and legs in a desperate attempt to escape death, which is to say the other soldier, who standing above him, lifts his arms high before planting his dagger squarely in the throat of his enemy. It is scarcely possible to describe the rich diversity of Leonardo's designs for the soldier's clothing, helmets, and ornaments, and the incredible mastery evidenced in the forms and silhouettes of the horses, whose musculature and elegant beauty has never been captured with such vigor by any other master." It is easy to understand Vasari's enthusiasm when one learns of the application with which Leonardo made anatomical drawings of humans and horses—of muscles, faces, and everything else. At this time, Leonardo, who was no longer young, continued to behave rather haughtily, making no effort to disguise his pride and his knowledge of his worth. He remained uncapturable. The prince's representative in Florence, Piero Soderini, saw nothing but insolence in one of Leonardo's noblest gestures. The artist refused to accept one of the monthly payments due him, which Soderini had counted out in small coins, justifying himself with the remark: "I am not a painter one can pay in small change." He knew the extent of his own gifts.

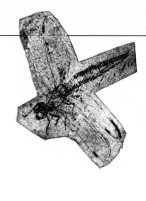

Leonardo had been observing birds for years. Their fantastic arabesques in the sky had always intrigued him. He wanted to realize man's long-standing dream to fly.

He first made a close study of the vulture, then of bats, which are in fact bird-like mammals. It seemed to him that they were the best acrobats of the air.

Given his fascination with birds and his penchant for drawing, it's not surprising that his notebooks are full of sketches of birds' wings. He conceived of the parachute. He also foresaw the helicopter.

Using the materials available to him—wire, glue, leather, steer horn, and cane—he built a flying machine. He gave careful consideration to movement, weight, and equilibrium, but he failed to take to the air in either 1498 or 1505. He who so loved birds that he wanted to become a bird-man found himself forever earthbound. But he had imagined how others who came after him, after a lapse of four centuries, would indeed be able to fly.

Of all his many devices, Leonardo probably invested the most creative energy in his flying machine. Flight appealed to something deep-seated in him. Remember that his earliest memory was of a vulture who came to his cradle. He could release birds from their cages, but he himself would never manage to join them in the air.

Studies of dragonflies and flying machines.

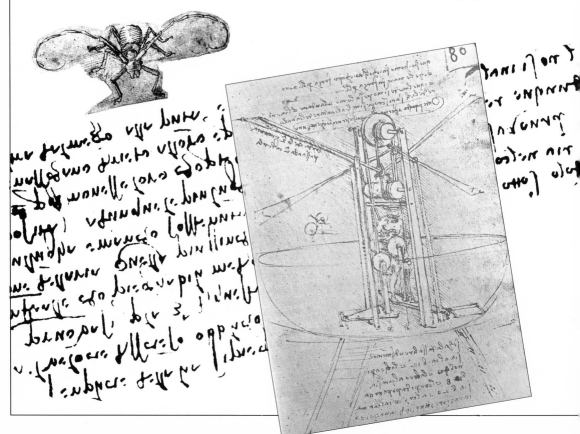

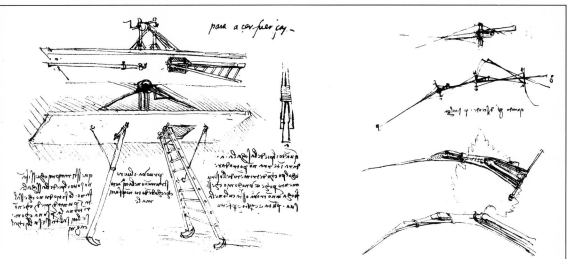

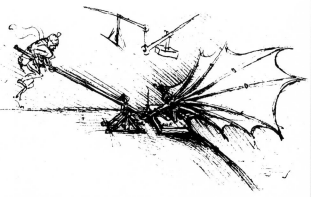

After birds and flight, it was water that most fascinated Leonardo, for water was capable of overflowing its banks and inundating the world, as the Arno River sometimes did. His projects for canals and containment systems reveal his considerable gifts as an engineer—an engineer who was always first and foremost a painter.

Rosa, it might well be that Leonardo, who had figured out so many things, knew how to make broken legs heal faster. I haven't been able to find anything about this in his writings, but then while several 1,000 pages of them have come down to us, several 1,000 more have been lost.

Rosa, I send my best regards to your imprisoned toes.

Your uncle Leo

P.S. Nothing now survives of *The Battle of Anghiari*, but if you want to get a better idea of it, you can find a reproduction of Rubens' copy of it.

Studies of flying machines.

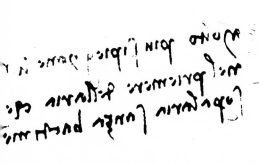

Dear uncle,

It's done. I've bought a sketch-book. So I'm sketching, which only makes sense. Doesn't it? I also bought a musical notebook, even though I can't read a note! I decided it would make a fine diary. Every day I write my secrets, big ones and little ones, on its staves. I have some things to say about you in it. But it's my private diary, so I'll keep them to myself.

I forgot: Parla italiano? Si? No? Just mark out the wrong answer.

If Leonardo were with me in this garden, I'd ask him to paint me. Perhaps he'd say yes, if only he could see my flush cheeks. If so, I'd take a

fragile branch in my hand. Since both my legs have been encased in plaster, I've felt rather fragile myself.

Rosa

P.S.: My legs in their plaster cases remind me of egg rolls.

The Virgin and Child with Saint Anne (1510).

Rosa-Lisa,

T he moment has finally arrived. We're going to talk about your friend Mona Lisa. You've learned a great deal about Leonardo and his work, so now let's turn our attention to the most famous painting in the world. I repeat: the most famous painting in the world! No small thing!

But let's also talk a bit about the *Virgin and Child with Saint Anne*, which is just as beautiful. In these two paintings, which were made in the last part of Leonardo's life, we find all the delicacy and subtle vibrancy that only Leonardo could capture.

The Virgin and Saint Anne both have smiles like the *Mona Lisa*, though they seem a bit less calculating. Both these women are beautiful, and they seem to be about the same age. But Saint Anne is the grandmother of Christ and the mother of Mary. They appear to be more beautiful than other saints because their beauty is presented to us straightforwardly and without exaggeration. Their lack of solemnity makes them seem more accessible. They play as though they were

Study.

Detail.

two ordinary women with an ordinary child. But such is not the case. Mary probably foresees a painful future. Leonardo's art has somehow transformed color and space into a representation of love. The compositional organization is basically pyramid-shaped, but with a spiral twist to give it movement. The complex interaction of the three bodies conveys the chain of love connecting Anne, Mary, and Jesus. The three exposed feet of the two women seem so soft and vulnerable that we want to caress them, warm them, protect them from the hard stone on which they rest. The rocky landscape in the distance is forbidding; we sense danger in it. Saint Anne could almost be Mona Lisa's twin sister.

The French call her *La Joconde*, the Italians *La Gioconda*, and Anglo-Saxons *Mona Lisa*, but whatever her name she remains an enigma. Painted between 1503 and 1507, the work is reputedly a portrait of Lisa Antonio Maria di Noldo Gherardini, the wife of Francesco di Bartolomeo di Lanobi del Giacondo. But there is some doubt about this. When Leonardo painted her she would have been 26. It is difficult for us today to see this work clearly: it has been so often reproduced on dish cloths and napkins, on calendars and in books, and so frequently manipulated by talented artists (Marcel Duchamp, who added a moustache and a few letters of the alphabet in 1919, being the first) and in clever advertising campaigns! And yet this work of pure painting remains inexhaustible. The woman's great beauty is intensified by the late-afternoon light, which falls sensuously over her serene face. But it makes her flesh positively vibrate. In this painting, Leonardo achieved something astounding: the complete fusion of light and life. Night falls in the distance. The landscape's rocky outcroppings delineate a place of death where ancient human fears reside. It is a desolate spot into which Leonardo introduces a redeeming love—imposing upon it, painting against it this woman who would be the work's only sun, whose presence holds back the night that wants to fall. Far from her being, nature is extinguished. In this landscape, she alone exhibits life in all its fullness. The painting, in its richness and multiplicity, is an image of Leonardo himself.

Mona Lisa (1503–1507).

She is kindness itself.
She is a lullaby.
She is a caress.
She is perhaps also a bit weary.
She participates in all of life's joys.
And is acquainted with its pains as well.

It is said that Leonardo, to make sure she was happy, surrounded her with musicians, singers, and clowns while he painted. He understood just how momentous a gesture it was to offer one's image to posterity. She doubtless had some sense of how her beauty would be manipulated by the artist's talent and intuition. Leonardo painted Mona Lisa's own smile, but at the same time he painted the smile of a child, of himself as a child. And a mother's smile that, while offering sweet comfort, cannot solve any of life's riddles. In painting Mona Lisa, he represented not only her but himself as well. In looking at the work we sense this. She is in a three-quarter pose. We see her hands and her hint of a smile that has the lightness of a wispy summer cloud. With the *Mona Lisa*, Leonardo takes us beyond mere appearances. He clutches us in an amorous embrace.

Let me explain myself, Rosa my Rose.

When we contemplate paintings by Leonardo like the *Mona Lisa* or the *Virgin and Saint Anne* or the *Virgin of the Rocks*, something similar

Marcel Duchamp, *L.H.O.O.Q.* (1919).

Fernand Leger, *Mona Lisa of the Keys* (1930).

happens: we lose ourselves in them. They transport us into a domain where love can flourish. Flawless perspective constructions that are not imbued with a similar longing or quest for insight are but illusions, nothing but empty show.

Fernando Botero, *Mona Lisa* (1978).

Leonardo never stopped asking questions about the source of life and its mysterious heart, which is love.

Your uncle Leo

P.S.: Don't worry too much about your legs healing. At your age, all should go well. But as for drawing your toes, that's another matter. Leonardo made the following recommendations about drawing the feet: "Apply to the feet the same rule you used for the hands, which is to say draw the muscles from six points of view, namely from behind and in front, above and below, inside and outside."

Dear uncle,

*H*ow lucky you are to be able to write so well about painting! And how lucky I am to be able to read what you write!

Why are you a poet and not a painter?

You know, if I see someone in the street, at the store, or wherever who looks like she could be the sister of Saint Anne or Mona Lisa, I'll give her your address and telephone number. But I intend to keep the words of your letters for myself. They're the most beautiful words in the world. So long as a ravishing Giaconda doesn't come along to spice up your life and your dreams, I will be the guardian of your words.

Keep writing.

Your eager-reader Rosa

Saint John the Baptist (1513–1516).

Dear Rosa,

The Chateau of Clos-Lucé.

Leonardo, as you know, was the pinnacle of painting. His exceptional gifts were widely acknowledged in his time, but it's also true that comparable praise was often bestowed on mediocrities who were nowhere near his level of achievement. Leonardo's amiability and studious courtesy made him easy to like, but those who loved him had to accept his rebellious streak, his tendency to resist taking orders.

I've told you a great deal, but now it's up to you to visit the museums, read books, and seek out information about Leonardo wherever you can. My letters could have been much longer. I could have written about Leonardo's passion for anatomy, which led him to ignore the prejudices of his time against dissecting the human body. I could have enumerated more of the machines he devised, more of his visionary plans and projects. And I could have asked you to follow him to Piombino on the Tuscan coast, to Venice (whose bankers were as renowned as those of Florence), and to Siena, Rimini, and Arezzo. Finally, I could have sketched a portrait of Leonardo's work as a military engineer for Cesare Borgia.

But I've written mostly about his painting. For him, painting was the ultimate endeavor. He ranked it much higher than poetry or music. That is what his *Saint John the Baptist,* with his mysterious smile and his finger pointing towards the heavens, seems to be telling us. This was Leonardo's final masterpiece.

Rosa, I think you now have a better sense of the benefits to be gained from looking closely. There is always more to see, more to learn. Soon you will able to move about freely in the world once more. Maybe you'll take a trip to the valley of the Loire River, which is just as unpredictable as the Arno in Florence. If so, be sure to go to Amboise. There you can see a beautiful example of French Renaissance architecture: the ancient manor house at Cloux, which is now known as Clos-Lucé. It was there that Leonardo spent his last years. At the end of 1516, accompanied by his students Salai and Francesco Melzi, he left Italy and crossed the Alps. After three months of traveling on the back of a mule, he reached the banks of the Loire. He had been invited there by his new protector Francis I, King of France. Leonardo settled into the house at Cloux with his paintings, drawings, manuscripts, and books. He was named "First Painter, Architect, and Engineer to the King."

He died on May 2, 1519.

It was appropriate for him to have died in spring, when the nature he so loved was at its peak. Leonardo's genius had helped banish many of man's worst fears and infused life with a new energy.

Your uncle Leo

Chronology

1452	Leonardo is born in Vinci on April 15. Natural son of Ser Piero di Antonio and Catarina.
1469	Settles with his family in Florence.
1472	Joins the Florentine painters guild.
1472–1476	Works in Verocchio's studio. Paints the left angel in his master's *Baptism of Christ*.
1478	Commissioned to paint an altarpiece for the Chapel of San Bernardo in the Palazzo della Signoria.
1480	Commissioned to paint a work for the church of the Brothers of San Donato in Scopeto, near Florence. This was the *Adoration of the Magi*, which was never completed.
1482	Settles in Milan. Offers his services to Ludovico il Moro.
1483	Begins to make studies for the equestrian statue of Francesco Sforza.
1487	Develops designs for the lantern of Milan Cathedral.
1490	Designs sets and costumes for a performance mounted on the occasion of the marriage of Isabella of Aragon and Gian Galeazzo Sforza.
1495	Begins work on *The Last Supper*. Paints *Woman with an Ermine*.
1499	Resides in Mantua at the court of Isabella d'Este.
1501	In Florence once more, executes the first studies for *Virgin and Child with Saint Anne* and *Saint John the Baptist*.
1502	Appointed military engineer to Cesare Borgia.
1503	Begins fresco of *The Battle of Anghiari* in the Palazzo Vecchio.
1507	In Milan, paints *Mona Lisa* and *Saint John the Baptist*, commissioned by Louis XII of France.
1508	Scientific and hydraulic studies.
1513	Settles in Rome; becomes the protege of Giulio di Medici.
1513–1515	Optical and anatomical studies.
1516	Invited by Francis I, King of France, to settle in the Chateau of Cloux.
1519	Dies at Cloux on May 20. Interred in the cloister of the Church of Saint-Florentin in Amboise.

When in Florence

How can one make recommendations about this city with a thousand seductions?

How can one describe its wonders after so many artists and writers have left accounts of this city in which so much was achieved, so many things invented?

The best advice one can give is: Try to rediscover the spirit of the Quattrocento when visiting it.

For in Florence, the curious will find that every street corner can become a new world.

Where Are the Works by Leonardo?

p. 12: Top: Prints and Drawings Department, Uffizi Gallery, Florence
Bottom: Library of the Institut de France, Paris
p. 13: Library of the Institut de France, Paris
pp. 15–16: Uffizi Gallery, Florence
p. 17: Top: Royal Library, Turin
p. 18: Alte Pinakothek, Munich
p. 19: National Gallery of Art, Washington
p. 20–21: Uffizi Gallery, Florence
p. 21: Bottom: Louvre Museum, Paris
pp. 22–25: Louvre Museum, Paris
pp. 26–27: Accademia, Venice
p. 31: Czartorisky Museum, Cracow
p. 32: Top: Ufizi Gallery, Florence
Bottom: British Museum, London
p. 33: Uffizi Gallery, Florence
p. 34: Prints and Drawings Department, Uffizi Gallery, Florence
p. 35: Prints and Drawings Department, Uffizi Gallery, Florence
p. 36: Convent of Santa Maria des Grazie, Milan
pp. 38–41: Convent of Santa Maria des Grazie, Milan
p. 45: Convent of Santa Maria des Grazie, Milan
p. 48: Accademia Gallery, Venice
p. 50: Upper left: Royal Palace, Turin
Bottom: Library of the Institut de France, Paris
p. 52: Louvre Museum, Paris
p. 55: Louvre Museum, Paris
p. 58: Louvre Museum, Paris

Photographic Credits

GLOSSARY

Baudelaire, Charles (1821–1867): greatest French poet of the 19th century and also a noted art critic.

Botticelli, Sandro (1445–1510): one of the greatest painters of the early Italian Renaissance.

Caravaggio, Michelangelo da (1573–1610): great painter of the Italian Renaissance known for his dramatic compositions and notorious lifestyle.

Duchamp, Marcel (1887–1968): one of the towering figures of 20th-century painting; known primarily for his sense of humor and the playful irreverence of much of his later work.

last supper: the last meal shared by Jesus with his disciples; celebrated by Christians in the sacrament of the Eucharist and depicted in many famous paintings.

Michelangelo (1475–1564): Italian sculptor, painter, poet, and architect of the late Italian Renaissance; the heir to Leonardo da Vinci as the greatest artist of his age.

middle ages: the period in European history from approximately A.D. 500 to 1500.

Petrarch, Francesco (1304–1374): Italian poet and statesman; greatest Italian poet after Dante.

Rembrandt Harmensz van Rijn (1606–1669): Dutch painter whose dark, shadowy portraits are among the greatest ever produced.

Renaissance: the period between the middle ages and modern times, usually dated between the 14th and 17th centuries; known for its great achievements in art, literature, and science.